Acquiring Rental Property

Learning Your Options for Starting Your Investment Portfolio

C.R. Wesley

C.R. Wesley

Acquiring Rental Property: Learning Your Options in Starting Your Investment Portfolio
Copyright © 2020 by C.R. Wesley

All rights. No portion of this book may be reproduced, stored in a retrieval system, or transmitted in any form or by any means – electronic, mechanical, recording or otherwise – except for brief quotation in printed reviews without the prior written permission of the publisher or the author.

C.R. Wesley

Disclaimer

The information contained in this literature is offered for informational purposes solely, and it is geared towards providing exact and reliable information regarding the topic and issue covered. The author and the publisher do not warrant that the information contained in this literature is fully complete. Some may be inclined to take alternate steps.

The author and publisher shall have neither liability nor responsibility to any person or entity concerning any reparation, damages, or monetary loss caused or alleged to be caused directly or indirectly by this literature. Therefore, this literature should be used as a guide - not as the ultimate source.

The publication is sold with the idea that the publisher is not required to render accounting, officially permitted or otherwise, qualified services. If advice is necessary, legal, or professional, a practiced professional should be ordered.

In no way is it legal to reproduce, duplicate, or transmit any part of this document in either electronic means or printed format. Recording of this publication is strictly prohibited, and any storage of this document is not allowed unless with written permission from the publisher. All rights reserved.

The author owns all copyrights not held by the publisher. The trademarks that are used are without any consent, and the publication of the trademark is without permission or backing by the trademark owner. All trademarks and brands within this literature are for clarifying purposes only and are not affiliated with this document.

For information contact :
(info@macroinvestmentsllc.com, http://www.macroinvestmentsllc.com)
Book and Cover design by Designer
ISBN: 9798747680388
Second Edition: May 2021

Table of Contents

Disclaimer — ii

Introduction — 1

Chapter 1 - *Becoming an Investor* — 6

Chapter 2 - *Aligning Your Financial Assistance* — 14

Chapter 3 - *Traditional Financing* — 41

Chapter 4 - *Non-Traditional Financing* — 48

Chapter 5 - *How to Leverage Money* — 52

Chapter 6 - *Knowing Your Numbers* — 66

Chapter 7 - *Finding Property* — 82

Chapter 8 - *Depreciation and Taxes* — 95

Chapter 9 - *Exit Strategy* — 100

Conclusion — 105

Introduction

Congratulations!

You are seeking the knowledge to become a better investor! Maybe you have already acquired property and you are now ready to make your second investment, which now makes you an investor! Keep up the good work! I congratulate you for seeking the knowledge, taking action and getting to this step! Knowledge is powerful, but the power of knowledge is in the action. We strive to keep you in action and motivated! If you haven't purchased a home before and you are looking to see how down payment assistance can be acquired along with the purchase process, be sure to check out the first issue of our Real Estate Knowledge Series, Securing Grant Money for First Time Home-Buyers by C.R. Wesley.

This issue teaches you how eligible buyers can receive down payment assistance in conjunction with their first home purchase. The two processes go "hand in hand"...Securing Grant Money for First Time Homebuyers by C.R. Wesley displays the entire buying process, proper preparation, and the appropriate steps to finding and receiving your down payment assistance or grants.

Now, back to the topic of discussion. According to experienced real estate investors, the difference between a rental property being a profitable investment and being a disaster is how much work an investor is willing to do. Anyone buying rental properties must choose properties that generate a positive cash flow, and this involves more than just the rent covering the mortgage payment.

It is a mistake for someone buying rental properties to think that they can deal with negative cash flow and just wait for the property to go up in value in order to sell for profit. Proper assessment must be done to see how the investment will perform in order to make an informed decision. Just ask those who purchased property in 2007 and then tried to sell their property in 2008 or 2009. It is normal that people may have the tendency to make mistakes, such as under estimating expenses. We are here to teach you the techniques to evaluate so you do not make these mistakes. Sometimes people expect to put no money down and get instant riches while also not screening prospective tenants. Do not be hasty with your actions regarding investments. Due diligence in all aspects are vitally important to your success. Calculate your actions and be sure strategic action-plans are set-up throughout the life of your investment.

It is important to understand that buying rental property is a long term investment. There are specific factors and basic rules to consider when you want to acquire a rental property.

In this literature, you will find out the various ways of acquiring investment property and you will also learn the details of how to analyze a prospective rental property. Every good plan has a plan after the original plan. Therefore, we will also review planning an exit strategy. Knowing your investment options is the first step. Take a close evaluation of what you can implement into your life. Finding the best investment strategy that fits your lifestyle is important. As you read through the options in this literature think about what you can realistically apply.

Upcoming literatures in the series will be:

✝ Understanding Tax Lien and Tax Deed Investing - No Fluff Book 3

by C.R. Wesley

These will help you correlate the best applicable strategy for your lifestyle or comfort level. Stay tuned...

Let us get started!

Chapter 1

Becoming an Investor

Becoming a real estate investor is not as difficult as you think even though you may not have the capital and experience. Sounds too good to be true, right? There are many ways of getting started in real estate investing. One of the easier, and getting more popular ways, is to become a bird dog.

> **_Definition of Real Estate Bird Dog_**
> *"Bird dog" is a real estate investing term that refers to someone who spends their time trying to locate properties with substantial investment potential. Generally, the intent is to find properties that are distressed and selling at a discount that can be repaired or remodeled and sold for a sizable profit.*

This is a method that can get you started by learning to target good real estate investments with a team of seasoned investors. A bird dog looks for motivated sellers or undervalued properties with the intention to pass the deal on to an investor. As you can imagine, the investor will have many questions for you to find out why you think this investment is ideal and has a sizable profit margin. Through these exchanges, your eye for ideal properties will improve.

For this exchange, the bird dog either charges a percentage of the profits or a flat fee to the real estate investor. Bird dogs work as an intelligence network for real estate investors. Real estate investors may work with a network of bird dogs to increase the coverage area of where they are looking for real estate deals. Similarly, a bird dog will also develop a network of real estate investors, so the bird dog has a better chance of converting the lead into a deal. The term bird dog is commonly associated with identifying properties for flipping, but it may also apply to identifying income properties for cash flow.

You should consider real estate bird dogging as the first step of your investing career if you are serious about becoming a real estate investor. Why? Because real estate investment requires you to have the knowledge and experience in addition to sufficient capital. This is an ideal role or second job for a beginning investor. While you are saving up for your next investment you could be obtaining vast knowledge as well.

As a real estate bird dog, you also get the opportunity to expose yourself to real estate investments without buying the properties. It is basically a risk free method of real estate investing where you will learn a lot. Depending on how much effort you are willing to put in, a bird dog can easily make a few hundred to a few thousand dollars a month by finding profitable deals for investors. You will defintely sharpen your communication and networking skills during the process. This education is ideal and will help your ability to become a seasoned investor.

Now back to acquiring your second property or investment property. Even if you have not acquired your second property yet, this next scenario may apply to you. Maybe you have purchased your first home and now you are renting it out (or a portion of it) for income or otherwise known as "house hacking".

🏆 *Nice job executing if so...Way to be creative!*

Or maybe you are preparing to purchase your second property, which from a lender's standpoint, deems you an investor being that the next purchase will not be your primary residence. Your second purchase of real estate, if not a second primary residence or eligible vacation home, now deems the purchase an investment property.

⚠ Be certain to not claim a second home if it is not in fact your second home. By law, lenders do not permit inaccurate residency status upon application of a loan. You will become liable for any legal consequences if you falsely classify your plans of residency.

When you reach your second property purchase, traditional lending will require you make a minimum down payment of 20% to 25%. If you are using non-traditional funding, you may qualify for up to 100% of the purchase price but most commonly a maximum qualification of 70-90% LTV (loan to value) is available. Some non-traditional lenders will lend based upon after repair value or ARV. In these cases, you have lenders that will lend at 65-75% of ARV including repairs.

For access to non-traditional lending and traditional lending, you will need to be prequalified. For traditional lending, you will be evaluated personally and for most non-traditional lending the asset will be evaluated. Either way, if you or the asset is being evaluated, you will have to qualify. With the prequalification, the lender will supply you with a proof of funds letter to show their support for your ability to purchase a property. A good investor identifies a good cash flowing property which could be at a good discount compared to market value or if the property has a high potential for increased value after renovation.

If you intend to be a part time or full time real estate investor, please be reminded that there are no quick bucks in real estate investing without thorough education. It is crucial that you treat real estate investing as a business. It may take months if not years for your business to bring in significant cash flow. Be sure to plan accordingly.

Do not give up your current occupation to become a real estate investor if you are not ready financially and have not developed adequate knowledge and experience. Again, being a bird dog is a great way to start your investing education. Otherwise, you are making a wise choice to seek the knowledge on how to acquire rental property by reading this literature. Remember, there are many options you can strategize to become an investor. An acquisition of a real estate purchase can come from various methods. As mentioned, we cover other methods of acquiring real estate in our Real Estate Knowledge Series. Upcoming literatures in the series will be Understanding Tax Lien and Tax Deed Investing – No Fluff (Book 3) by C.R. Wesley. These will help you correlate the best applicable investment strategy for your lifestyle or comfort level. Stay tuned...

Chapter 2

Aligning Your Financial Assistance

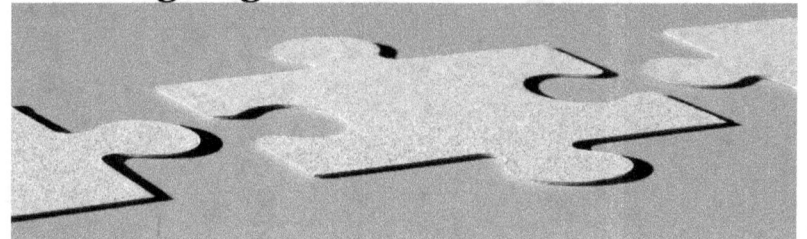

Locating and understanding the right financing is a critical piece to the real estate investor's puzzle because many of us do not have the money to purchase a property for all cash. Most of us will need to borrow a major portion of the purchase from a lender whether private or from an institution. You should review your financial stability before making any investments. Take precaution so you are well prepared. The primary reasons many businesses get into trouble and encounter problems are listed below:

- ✓ **Not enough cash flow.**
    - *Example – The property you have chosen to purchase has expenses that you did not account for in your cash flow analysis causing your investment to have low or negative cash flow.*
    - *Example – A property you are selling is pending and has not sold, so you do not have the cash to pay the mortgage on an unoccupied property this month.*
- ✓ **Bad Accounting.**
    - *Example - In a lucrative year, you owe the IRS $30,000 but only have $18 left in your business bank account. This has put you into debt due to not adequately preparing for expenses.*

- ✓ **Poor Management.**
  - *Example - Your bookkeeping plan is chaotic or nonexistent. Your ability to keep track of your current and future state of business is absent.*
  - *Example – Your property management company is not communicating well and making decisions without involving you. Causing you to go cash flow negative whether it be from ineffective repair decisions, high vacancy rates or ineffective people skills to create an effective relationship with tenants.*

These are examples to keep in mind so you prepare effectively. A large portion of being prepared is your ability to evaluate the deal. This involves a good cash flow analysis procedure. This is where good bookkeeping is involved, so start good habits now. In aligning our financial assistance, we must first understand if the deal is worth pursuing and presentable to the lender. To determine this, we need to complete a cash flow analysis.

Create and verify your cash flow analysis carefully to see how a prospective property will perform in the future. This is an important step. To evaluate your properties, you should gather the data and conduct a cash flow analysis.

A cash flow analysis helps you to figure out whether your investment is cash flow positive or cash flow negative. The rate of the positive cash flow helps you determine how good your investment really is and if you should pursue the investment.

We will present the example and then define a few key terms before showing the cash flow analysis chart.

Below is a general cash flow analysis example.

EXAMPLE

Note: The figures in this example will be used throughout the text in various investment evaluation techniques.

In this example we have a (2) unit (duplex) property with a purchase price of $150,000. It is occupied and has rental income of $2,400 per month and parking income of $150 per month.

We will use the industry standard vacancy rate of 5%. This standard accounts for typical transition time between tenants.

> *Vacancy Rate Definition* - *The vacancy rate is the percentage of all available units in a rental property, such as a hotel or apartment complex, that are vacant or unoccupied at a particular time. A vacancy rate is the opposite of the occupancy rate, which is the percentage of units in a rental property that are occupied.*

Operating expenses can include property taxes, management fees, snow removal or lawn care, maintenance, insurance, scavenger/trash, water/sewer, extermination, electricity, gas/oil, capital expenses (Cap X), supplies, legal fees, salary, advertising, inspections, janitorial/cleaning, reserves and accounting.

> *Operating Expenses Definition* - *Operating expenses are ongoing costs to maintain and keep a rental property investment in service. Typically, they represent a huge financial chunk of what real estate investors must pay to own rental property and ultimately play a major role in the real estate investment decision.*

Be mindful of all your applicable operating expenses and plan accordingly. Depending on the property and your business plan, you may not need to account for all possible operating expenses. Typically, smaller properties with lower units may not need the same operating expenses required for larger properties with several units. For example, a 5-unit property may not have a salaried maintenance person as a 100-unit property would. We will dive deeper into operating expense types later in the text so you can brainstorm on the possible expenses you would account for. For now, let us place our (2) unit property and its operating expenses into our cash flow analysis table to see if this property is cash flow positive. In this example, we will qualify the property as not needing any substantial repairs outside of yearly preventative maintenance. To currently simplify the details in this example, all operating expenses have been summarized. We will review line item detail for operating expenses later in the literature.

CASH FLOW ANALYSIS TABLE

(2) Units @ $1200 per month each

(2) Garages @ $75 per month each

CASH FLOW ANALYSIS		
Purchase Price	$	150,000
Gross Income (Monthly)	$	2,550
Gross Income (Annual)	$	30,600
Vacancy Rate 5%	$	1,530
Effective Gross Income	**$**	**29,070**
Annual Mortgage (or Debt Service)	$	8,892
Annual Taxes	$	1,612
Annual Insurance	$	951
Annual Operating Expenses	$	10,175
Total Operating Expenses (w/ Debt Service)	**$**	**21,630**
Cash Flow (before income taxes)	**$**	**7,440**
C.R. Wesley		

Note: To keep the example simple, we did not go into depth with line item detail for each of the operating expense types. Normally your analysis table would display the expense types for clarity.

So, what do you think? Good investment? Bad investment? Should we approach the lender for support in purchasing?

- Yes - this is a good investment. This property is cash flow positive and producing $7,440 per year before income taxes. 👍

    Cash Flow Definition - Cash flow is the profit made from a rental property. This figure is prior to income taxes.

- Per month, this equates to $620 or $310 per unit.

- Additionally, the cash on cash return for this investment is 19.84%. 👍

    Cash on Cash Return Definition - Cash-on-cash return measures the annual return the investor made on the property in relation to the down payment only and is calculated as: Cash-on-cash return only uses an investment property's pre-tax inflows received *by the investor and the pre-tax outflows paid by the investor.*

📇 Cash on Cash Return is the cash flow divided by the cash down payment for the investment.

✍ **Note:** The down payment for this example is 25% of $150,000 or $37,500.

($7,440 divided by $37,500 equals 0.1984 or 19.84%)

🧮 **Cash on Cash Return = Cash Flow/Down Payment**

A cash flow analysis includes operating activities, investing activities and financial activities. A cash flow analysis does not take into consideration depreciation or income taxes.

Investors use the information in a cash flow analysis to determine a rate of return or the overall capitalization rate. In this example the cash on cash return is 19.84% which is a good investment.

To consider the overall capitalization rate or CAP rate, the net operating income (NOI) is divided by the purchase price. We will delve more into the investment analysis equations later in the literature. For now, let us complete the topic of aligning your financial assistance now that we see this (2) unit property is a good investment based on the cash flow and the cash on cash return percentage.

Now let us begin to discuss mortgage types. We will first start with options available on how the interest is accumulated during the life of the loan. The mortgage types available include fixed-rate mortgages, adjustable rate mortgages and interest-only mortgages. These mortgage types specifically relate to how the interest accumulates. You will need to choose the right type of loan for your plan. This is a good starting point, but there are more details, regarding loan types, than just how the interest accumulates based upon the mortgage type, so keep that in mind. We will review traditional lending options and non-traditional lending options. First let us look at the mortgage packages as they relate to interest.

You may want a more stable mortgage type and decide to choose a fixed rate loan where finances are consistent for the life of the loan. This eliminates some of the risk involved in the investment. Adjustable rate mortgages can change the property from a good investment to a bad investment if the interest rates skyrocket. You also have the choice of an interest-only mortgage. Interest only mortgages are often used to maximize cash flow for the disclosed term that the loan will be payable by interest only. When this term ends, usually the mortgage payments will increase due to the loan transferring to an adjustable rate mortgage. The loan terms will depend on the loan package chosen since there are many optional terms. You can establish the best plan suitable for you. Below we will outline the financing options as it relates to interest. These mortgage options only apply to how the interest accumulates. We will go further into traditional and non-traditional loan types later in the chapter. Regardless of the loan type, you will have to decide the type of mortgage you prefer.

Here are more details on the mortgage types as it relates to interest accumulation.

Mortgage Types & Interest

☞ **Fixed Rate Mortgage** - Fixed-rate mortgages keep the same interest rate over the life of the loan, which means your monthly mortgage payment will always stay the same. Fixed rate loans typically come in terms of **10 years**, **15 years**, 20 years, 25 years and **30 years**.

☞ **Adjustable Rate Mortgages** – Adjustable rate mortgages (ARMs) have fluctuating interest rates that can go up or down with market conditions. Many ARM products have a fixed interest rate for a few years before the loan resets to a variable interest rate for the remainder of the term - usually adjusted yearly.

☞ **Interest Only Mortgages** – For interest only mortgages the borrower only pays the interest for a fixed term and then either pays the loan off or they begin an adjustable rate term for the remainder of the new term length. Be mindful that during the interest only period, the principal is not being paid so the initial principal loan amount is still due at the end of the interest only term. Interest only terms are usually periods between 3 and 10 years. After the interest only period is over either a balloon payment is due (symbolizing the remaining principal) or you would begin paying off the principal with an adjustable rate-interest mortgage for the remainder of the term, usually 25 or 30 years.

Non-Traditional Lenders and Interest Rates

Non-traditional lenders and their interest rate options are much simpler as it relates to package options. The rates applied to a non-traditional lending package are first determined by the purchasing plan.

1) If you are using a renovation package, you will have a short-term interest only mortgage. The loan can vary from 6 months to 36 months of interest only payments and then the principal loan amount is due at the end of the term. This gives you time to renovate

and resell or renovate and refinance into a long-term finance package. You would not want a mortgage that pays into principal because your renovation plan involves adding value. Therefore, you would want to minimize any debt during the renovation period and these loans are short term-interest only.

2) If you are using a purchase package, then your optional mortgage packages are like traditional lending packages, just with higher interest rates. These loans usually have more flexible qualifications for the acquisition due to the asset and the renovation plan being the determining factors.

Choice of Lending Sources

You have the choice of acquiring lending from either a banking institution, a hard money institution or a private money lender. We will review further details on each as we continue to display options on aligning your finances.

Banking Institution: Commercial banks are a traditional source of funding and have a real estate loan department available to assist you with their loan products. Some of the largest commercial banks are also involved in real estate financing through their trust department. These include mortgage banking operations and real estate investment trusts or REITS. A real estate investment trust (REIT) is a closed-end investment company that owns assets related to real estate such as buildings, land, and real estate securities. REITs sell on the major stock market exchanges just like common stocks.

- Banking institutions have several types of loans to fit your investment strategy. There are two initial classifications – residential loans and commercial loans.

- For investors, residential loans are Conventional, FHA and Jumbo Loans. More options are available for owner occupants, but we are only discussing investment purchases.
- Commercial loans are Interest Only Loans, Refinance Loans, Bridge Loans, Construction Loans and Blanket/Portfolio Loans.

Here are a few requirements when borrowing from a traditional lender:

- Credit Check

- Bank Statements
- Tax Returns
- Proof of Business Registration
- Employer Identification Number
- Financial Statements (or W-2's)
- Pay stubs
- Details of Your Other Loans
- Subject Property Address
- Specified Length of Consistent Employment

Hard Money Lenders: Hard money lenders are a non-traditional lending source. Loans come from institutions or companies who lend money based on the property they are investing in, or what is considered, a collateral-based loan. These loans are usually simpler to acquire due to less requirements for underwriting. However, these purchases are through entities and they have the highest annual percentage rates or APRs. Entity examples are LLC's, C Corps, S Corps, LLP's etc...The borrower will need ownership of an entity to proceed.

- Hard money can be acquired for many types of purchases provided the property meets the lenders qualifications.
- Hard money loan types consist of:
    - Renovation Loans, Purchase Loans, Interest Only Loans, Refinance Loans, Bridge Loans, Gap Loans, Construction Loans and Blanket/Portfolio Loans.
- Hard money lenders are exclusively in the business of providing funding. Although, hard money may follow some of the same funding concepts as private money, the rates of borrowing are usually higher.

- Hard money loan rates usually range from 10% to 18% with three to 36-month terms. There are usually points paid upon closing that fall between 2% and 10% of the loan amount. Pricing is primarily based on risk, equity, and the borrower's experience.

Private Money Lenders: Private money lenders are a non-traditional source of funding and typically lend money based on the asset they are investing in, or what is considered, a collateral-based loan. Private money lenders can be anyone from a personal friend to an established private lending company. Therefore, they are often referred to as "relationship-based" lenders. Expect to be creative within this bracket of lenders. They are usually open to discuss any lucrative investment. Provided you are experienced and have a lucrative investment strategy, they may join you. Usually shorter-term returns are desired.

- Private lending can be any entity or individual that is willing to allow you to borrow funds for their specified rates and terms. Private lending can come from people putting their 401k funds together, capital from one individual willing to lend or several partnering individuals putting their capital together to lend. Private money loans come from a source that is not typically in the business of solely providing loans. Private money loan rates usually range from 5% on up...They usually have interests in various endeavors and lending is just a component of their business ventures.

Here are some tips in what you will need to consider for non-traditional lenders:

- Research and find a reliable lender.
- Consider the pros and cons of accepting the loan.
- Evaluate the time frame of your loan.
- Present the potential value of the property you want to purchase.
- Present a clear financial plan for your project.
- Possibly prepare additional documentation to support your investment proposal.
- Protect yourself legally by having your attorney review the terms of the loan before you sign anything.
- Remain in contact with the lender.
- Receive the loan.
- Move quickly on securing your investment.

- Prepare to cover closing costs or any additional underwriting fees for the loan.
- Secure property insurance.
- Pay back the loan after your business plan is executed.

Down Payment and Closing Time

Traditional financing institutions will require a minimum down payment of 20% to 25% for an investment property. They also require that the property is livable unless you are applying for a renovation loan like a 203k or the HomeStyle Renovation Loan. A 203k would not be optional in this scenario since 203k's are only eligible to owner occupants. However, the HomeStyle Renovation Loan is a renovation product you can utilize. You will need to find a lender who supports the program. This is a good program that can save you money on the interest rates if chosen. Banks usually take 30-60 days to close on a real estate transaction.

A Non-traditional lender can usually close in as little as 2 days and up to 3 weeks depending on the lender. Non-traditional lenders may or may not require a down payment. This will depend on their lending terms and possibly the investors experience. Usually non-traditional lenders become more flexible in their lending terms based upon the investors experience.

Remember that traditional lenders are lending based upon your credit worthiness and not only the asset. Therefore, you will be evaluated as well as the asset. Non-traditional lenders lend more based upon the asset and not your personal credit worthiness.

Due Diligence

The option of using a traditional or non-traditional lender is your choice. Your preference will relate to the investment opportunity, your capability, and your plan.

Choosing private money or hard money may provide you the flexibility to pursue and acquire more investments than traditional lending would. While adversely, traditional lending sources can save you substantially from lower interest rates, if the acquisition terms support it. Choose what best supports your business plan and comfort level. It is your responsibility to identify the lending choice that makes the most sense for the investment. In any regard, research any method and lender before applying for funding.

When choosing your lender, you will need to evaluate your financial responsibility by knowing all related fees, points, origination fees, closing costs and the APR on the borrowed money. In applying for funding, you will need to produce any applicable information upon the lenders request. In preparing for your purchase, be mindful of how much you are eligible to borrow and how much it will cost you to borrow the money. Conduct your interviews with any prospective lenders to ensure you are getting the best rates possible. It is good to have your attorney review your contracts before signing off.

Chapter 3

Traditional Financing

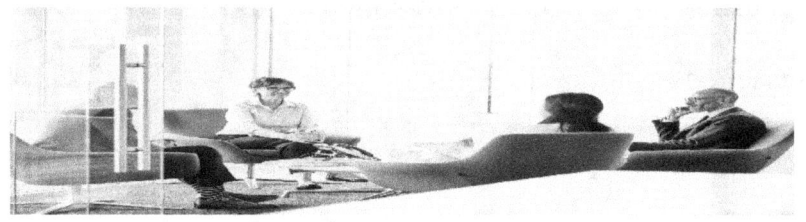

As mentioned, traditional financing is lending that is borrowed from a banking institution. Lending against the cash flow generated by the property is the most common form of real estate investing. Banking institutions lend on these types of investments most frequently. In it's simplest form, it involves a loan to a borrower which is repaid from the rental income of the borrower's property. It is the most commonly used structure for real estate investing.

Real estate finance transactions are usually classified as either investment or development transactions. The Loan Market Association has published standard form facility agreements for both investment and development transactions as follows:

- An Investment Facility Agreement—whereby a loan facility is provided to a borrower for it to purchase a property or a group of properties.
- A Development Facility Agreement—whereby a loan facility is provided to a borrower for it to purchase a property or group of properties as well as providing funds for the development of the property or properties.

Commercial and Residential Financing

Commercial real estate consist of office buildings, industrial buildings, multi-family properties (5 units or more) and retail buildings. These are usually repaid from the rent received from tenants known as commercial real estate financing.

> **Note:** *Any mixed-use properties are classified as commercial even if they are less than 5 units.*

Residential real estate investments are usually repaid from the sale of individual residential properties known as residential real estate financing. Residential properties are 1 to 4-unit residential properties.

Source for Traditional Financing

Online Mortgage Lenders

Chances are you have seen at least one advertising for Rocket Mortgage. Quicken Loans, which launched Rocket

Mortgage, represents one of the most substantial companies in a new generation of online mortgage lenders. Online lenders are offering consumers with mortgage and refinancing approvals in a matter of minutes, using loan-decision algorithms. These programs appeal widely to today's largest group of home buyers, who prefer to shop for products online.

Marketplaces and Brokers

Similar to the concept of online mortgage lenders, many popular websites such as Zillow or Lending Tree offer consumers a list of potential loan products to choose from. Once you enter your information, a search is performed by an algorithm that takes basic information entered by the shopper and matches nonconforming mortgage rates and products offered by lenders. The consumer then selects their preferred product and works directly with the lender to finish processing the application. In turn, these marketplaces and brokers, which can be thought of as middlemen, receive a fee for providing lenders with leads.

Within the traditional lending realm, there are several loans that may support your investment strategy. Be sure to evaluate any programs to verify the requirements and what the program entails.

Traditional Lending with Renovation Products

Homestyle Renovation Program is a traditional lending program that assists by aligning the resources you need if you want to renovate a single family or multi-family residence. These homes do not need to be in livable condition when purchased. This is a great option for those investors who prefer to use a traditional financing option but want to renovate and hold or resell. This program is like a 203k, but without the need to owner occupy. Follow up with your lender for details or seek out lenders who support this program.

> **<u>Defined</u>: HomeStyle Renovation Program** – *The HomeStyle Renovation program allows eligible borrowers to include financing for home improvements for a purchase or refinance transaction of an existing home. This program can only be used in conjunction with the HFA Preferred™ of the HFA Preferred Risk Sharing™ products. The total cost of the renovations, repairs or improvements cannot exceed 75% of the "as completed appraised value" after renovations are completed.*

- Be sure to check your states grant and resource directory for applicable programs that may provide support for some of your investments:

If you are not using the HomeStyle Renovation Loan, you will need to verify that your investment is in livable condition. This is required for a traditional lender to support the purchase under any loan package. If a property is already occupied with tenants, this could be a reliable investment for you to acquire using traditional lending. Consult with your lender of choice for details.

Chapter 4

Non-Traditional Financing

A non-conventional mortgage, is a type of loan product that does not conform to traditional mortgage loan requirements. Conventional loans have a common set of qualifications and eligibility requirements, such as credit scores, loan amounts and debt-to-income ratios. In addition, many conventional loans require a 20% to 25% minimum down payment along with private mortgage insurance. Non-conventional loans, can offer more flexible qualification terms. Often, they are more flexible due to being capable of a faster close with less of a down payment if any down payment at all. These loans are asset-based loans where the asset is the collateral. Therefore, the asset and your business plan play the highest role in loan approval.

Non-Institutional Lenders and Non-Traditional Lenders

Small lenders and credit unions provide an alternative to home buyers who have less than perfect credit. Because non-institutional entities often do not face as many federal regulations as their counterparts, they are able to provide more flexible options to consumers. As a result of the housing crisis, many big banks have decreased their roles in mortgage lending, limiting their products to the most qualified borrowers. In recent years, non-bank lenders have increasingly filled this void.

Within the non-traditional lending realm, you can purchase any property of choice (including land) provided you meet qualifications. An investment that makes sense is an investment that has the repair costs and the after repair value evaluated accurately and allows enough profit to warrant support from the lender. The more experience you have, the more leverage the lender will lend to you. Having a direct, well communicated strategy is essential. You will also need a "Plan B" in case things do not go as planned. With an established relationship with the lender you will be supported for your investment.

Sources for Non-Traditional Financing

Some of the places you can find non-traditional lenders for private and hard money loans include www.biggerpockets.com, www.connectedinvestors.com and your local REIA (Real Estate Investment Association) meetings.

A good source for finding local REIA's is www.meetup.com.

Chapter 5

How to Leverage Money

Real estate investing gets more exciting and potentially more rewarding when you make money with other peoples' money. That is where learning about investment property financing and real estate leverage comes in handy.

Leverage in real estate simply means how much money you borrow to finance an investment property compared to the property's worth. We use the term "leverage" because we are leveraging other people's money to maximize our ability to buy more investment properties with less of your own money. The higher your leverage, the higher your potential return on investment (ROI).

Leveraging money to make your purchase is key. Leveraged real estate investing can increase the profit margin on your investment properties. For example, let us say you have $50,000 cash on hand. You can use that money in four different ways if not more…See examples below.

- Buy a $50,000 investment property with all the cash you have on hand. This equals a 0% leverage.

- Buy a $100,000 investment property with the $50,000 cash you have on hand and use a lender to borrow $50,000. This equals a 50% leverage.

- Buy a $200,000 rental property using the $50,000 cash you have on hand and use a lender to borrow $150,000. This equals 75% leverage.

- Or buy two properties with $200k with $25k down on each property using the $50,000 cash you have on hand and use a lender to borrow $150,000. This also equals 75% leverage.

We often search for where we will find the funds to get our investments started. Well, there are several ways, which could be borrowing from your 401k, using a home equity line of credit (HELOC), getting a personal loan, using private money, using hard money or using your cash savings. Your 401K or a HELOC is the cheapest and suggested ways because the interest rates will be the lowest and you are not using your cash reserves. Cash reserves are best used as leverage to acquire property unless your preference is to not have a mortgage. Be prepared for the repayment schedule within any strategy you utilize.

🖩 To calculate leverage on your investment, simply divide your investment funds by the total funds financed.

🖩 To calculate loan to value, simply divide your financed amount by the property value. This is known as the loan-to-value ratio (LTV).

🖩 **Leverage = Funds Contributed/Total Funds Financed**

If we use our example, we know our dawn payment is $37,500 and the funds financed would be $112,500. Let us plug this into the equation to figure what our leverage is.

🖩 0.33 = $37,500/$112,500 or a 33.3% leverage position on your behalf, 67% from the lender.

🖩 **LTV = Total Funds Financed/Property Value**

Let us use our example to compute our LTV.

🖩 0.75 = $112,500/$150,000 or a 75% LTV

Leveraged real estate investing works best when rents and property values are rising. Appreciation is a key factor here. As rents and the value of the investment rise, their monthly mortgage for rental property remains constant, creating larger and larger profits through appreciation. In many areas, today's rents and property values are appreciating handsomely. This is the ideal environment for the investor who knows how to leverage investments with borrowed money.

Contemplate on our investment strategies to find the best applicable method for you. Many investors build their portfolio with rental properties in locations of low appreciation, but high cash flow. These are locations where cash flow is high, but property appreciation may be incredibly low or nonexistent. Investors can gain higher quantities of assets pursuing this method creating great cash flow. These properties tend to be lower cost due to the lack of appreciation. With higher cash flow this could allow you to pay down the mortgage faster. Do your due diligence as this may be a method you choose.

As similarly mentioned, another strategy is investing in an area where the property appreciates but has lower cash flow. In this example, your cash flow will be less, however your property will appreciate. These properties tend to be higher cost due to the trend of appreciation. With appreciation this could allow you to gain equity and refinance or sell the property for profit sooner. These prospective examples are classified into asset classes where the correlation of the investment type is given in respect to the asset class referenced. Asset class will be covered in Chapter 7 – Finding Property. Properties are generally classified as A Class, B Class, C Class and D Class.

As an application of evaluating when to pursue an investment and leverage your money, we will review a technique for evaluating the potential income for an investment. This is where you evaluate the net operating income on an investment. Let us first define net operating income, show our typical expense types and then proceed to our example chart. We will use the same (2) unit property example.

NOI Definition

Net operating income (NOI) is a calculation used to analyze the profitability of real estate investments that generate income. Net operating income equals all revenue from the property minus all necessary operating expenses. NOI is a before-tax, before debt figure that excludes principal and interest payments on loans, capital expenditures, depreciation, and amortization. This metric is also used in other industries but is called EBIT, or earnings before interest and taxes.

Be sure to consider all applicable expenses when calculating your operating expenses.

See reference chart below of applicable expenses.

Operating Expenses

Property Taxes
Management Fee
Vacancy Rate
Snow Removal/Lawn Maintenance
Property Insurance
Scavenger/Trash
Water/Sewer
Extermination
Electric
Gas Heat
Cap X
Supplies
Legal/Salary
Advertising
Inspection
Janitorial/Cleaning
Reserves
Accounting

☞ *Below is an example of evaluating your net operating income (NOI).*

Overall, net operating income (NOI) is a calculation used to analyze the profitability of an investment.

NET OPERATING INCOME (NOI) TABLE

NET OPERATING INCOME (NOI)	
Gross Income	**$ 30,600**
Vacancy Rate (5%)	$ 1,530
Effective Gross Income	$ 29,070
Other Income (Parking)	$ 1,800
Effective Gross Income	**$ 29,070**
Property Taxes	$ 1,612
Property Insurance	$ 951
Property Manager Fees @ 7%	$ 2,035
Other Operating Expenses	$ 8,140
Total Operating Expenses	**$ 12,738**
Net Operating Income (NOI)	**$ 16,332**
C.R. Wesley	

Net operating income equals all revenue from the property minus all operating expenses.

NOI = Effective Gross Income – Operating Expenses

$16,332 = $29,070 - $12,738

Note: *Effective gross income includes vacancy rate. Also, NOI does not include the mortgage (or debt service). (Cash flow does...)*

In this example, the investor would profit $16,332 per year before debt service and income taxes.

📢 To provide some insight, lenders look at how much the assets' income covers the debt service. This is called the debt service coverage ratio (DSCR). Lenders use this as an indicator for how well the asset can potentially perform.

📢 *TIP: Usually lenders will not lend on an asset with a debt service coverage ratio (DSCR) of less than 1.2. Usually at a DSCR of 1.35 your investment is beginning to look favorable.*

🖩 Debt Service Coverage Ratio (DSCR) equals the NOI divided by the annual debt service.

Acquiring Rental Property

🖩 DSCR = NOI/Annual Debt Service

Using the data, we have from Chapter 2, let us use our annual debt service amount to place into our DSCR equation and see where we land.

$$1.84 = \$16{,}332/\$8{,}892$$

👍 Nice! We are at a DSCR of 1.84!! 👍

This investment is looking quite favorable! Let us continue now that we know our net operating income.

<u>One of the next questions we should be asking ourselves is:</u>

- What type of asset are we looking to buy here?
- How is the neighborhood?
- Is the neighborhood on an economic incline or an economic decline?

<u>When reviewing properties, please get familiar with the area of the property and define if you are.</u>

1) Gaining assets that appreciate with less cash flow

2) Gaining assets with little to no appreciation that produce high cash flow.

3) Gaining assets with decent appreciation and decent cash flow.

> *Note: Be mindful that some investors face the risk of depreciating assets in selecting option 2. Meaning the value of their assets could decline over time although they are achieving high cash flow.*

Partner with your trusted professionals and inquire about this factor to see what the history is around your prospective purchase. This history reflects asset class and what the typical capitalization rate has been around your prospective investment. We will review this in the next chapter.

For now, calculate your strategy and research the locations you are investing in before entering an investment.

Be informed that your plan to gain equity can come from appreciation or from direct payments to principal. With a higher cash flow, it is very possible you can pay off the asset sooner than your planned financial term. Or with an appreciating asset, you could gain equity faster and anticipation to refinance or sell. This should be included in your exit plan.

A good rate of appreciation or a sign of a higher asset class is where an asset is achieving 3-5% (or more) in appreciation per year. These are considered locations with high rates of appreciation. A realtor or broker who knows the area well can help you determine this factor. Some locations do not appreciate at all or they appreciate little over long time spans. Again, beware that you run the risk of assets that may depreciate based upon location. Assess your prospective areas' potential in conjunction with your investment strategy before entering an investment.

Chapter 6

Knowing Your Numbers

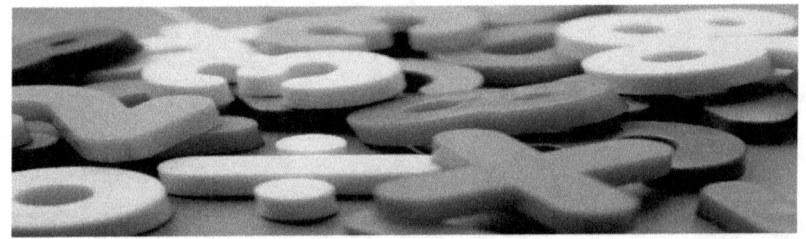

There is a lot that goes into evaluating a real estate investment. From what you have learned so far, you are equipped with the knowledge to gather and apply that information. As you can see there are several figures to gather. In addition, be prepared to do your due diligence and complete all general inspections necessary to confirm conditions throughout the property. If you are just getting started, it can be easy to get overwhelmed with the amount of information to collect and all the ratios, formulas and due diligence involved. However, with what you have learned so far, you can go and apply your knowledge taking calculated action! Keep up the good work!

While calculations may seem daunting and at times a little overwhelming, the reality is that, knowing these numbers are critical to your success. The more you practice them, the simpler they will become. There are several resources that you can seek out to help you with obtaining the tools to evaluate the numbers. www.biggerpockets.com has some great resources and calculators you can seek out. Or maybe you are great with Microsoft Excel and you will create your own tables and calculators...Just be sure you have a resource and you assess these details diligently. Whether you will complete this diligence yourself or if a member of your team will, it is vital to your success.

If you do not know where all the numbers come from, you are just taking a guess on the profitability of a property.

This is a very expensive gamble to take. Do not do this! If the numbers do not make sense, leave the deal alone. A bad investment can wipe away all the good things you have done with your business. The right numbers are important for every real estate transactions – no exceptions.

A cash flow analysis is an essential analysis to investigate. If you are using a buy and hold-long term strategy or a BRRRR-(Buy-Rehab-Rent-Refinance-Repeat)-short term strategy, your exit strategy is equally important to the entrance strategy. Consider your exit strategy being your second acquisition, with the first acquisition being the purchase of the property. Also do not forget inspections are also a part of your due diligence. Be sure you have a thorough due diligence process for any investment. Your due diligence plan should be supported in your agreement/paperwork with the seller.

The most common mistake overzealous investors make is missing key details causing the deal to appear like a good investment. Stick to a process of gathering all your numbers and cost assessments. Be conservative and do your homework on the area. Comparable rents and comparable property sales are important.

Due Diligence

Here are some vital assessments to establish on property conditions:

☞ *Roof* – When was the roof last replaced? Also, based on the roofing material, what is its life expectancy?

☞ *Electrical* – Is the electrical system up to date with enough circuits to accommodate the home?

☞ *Plumbing* (including well & septic if applicable) – Are there any plumbing issues? If so, what will it take to correct them?

☞ **Foundation** – Are there any foundation issues? If so, how much will it cost to repair the issue?

☞ **Individually Metered** – Is the gas and electric individually metered (and water if preferred) for each unit?

☞ **HVAC** – How old is the operating system and is it efficient? Will the system need replacing?

☞ Cosmetics- Kitchen/Bathrooms & Flooring

☞ Parking and curb appeal.

Even though you may like a property and see value in it, if the area comparable rents only yield $800/month and you need $1200 to meet profit margins, there is probably no amount of work you can do to get that number up to $1200. The consumer - in that area - is not looking to pay $400 extra. Under this scenario, you must increase your rehab/repair budget to try to get a rental amount that is not realistic in the first place. This is money that would be of better use on another worthwhile investment.

Be sure not to rely on old data or seller opinions as fact. Your comparables should be within 1 year and as close as possible to the property. Usually a comparable distance is within a mile but could go up to 3 or 5 miles from the property. In large metropolitan areas, you often want to target within 0.25 – 0.5 miles. Please refer to your real estate agent for confirmation on what comparable techniques are ideal for your market. Be sure all the comparables you use are from a reliable and validated source. Be sure to use the most recent data usually within present day to a year. Do your due diligence and find the most current and accurate comparables within a reliable distance from the prospective property.

Comparable Definition

> *Comparables (or comps) is a real estate appraisal term referring to properties with characteristics that are similar to a subject property whose value is being sought.*

Valuation

If you are forced to, estimate on the side of caution when aligning fair market value (FMV) or after repair value (ARV). Being more conservative with value may or may not make the property look as great, but it will give you a much more accurate depiction of the profitability of the property. It will also give you room for error which can happen in many forms. When planning for repairs, there are unexpected costs that occur frequently. This will also prepare you better for the worst-case scenario. There will be scenarios where unplanned expenses will arise.

It is important that you know all fees associated with any method of financing you plan. Calculate these related fees up through the expected pay off date into your evaluation. Here are some assessments you will need to verify and calculate in your evaluation.

Net operating income (NOI) and capitalization rates (CAP) are integral parts of valuating properties. Since we have already covered NOI, let us review CAP rate to see how it relates to analyzing valuation potentials.

<u>CAP Rate Definition</u>

Capitalization rate *(or "**cap rate**") is a real estate valuation measure used to compare different real estate investments. Although there are many variations, a cap rate is often calculated as the ratio between the net operating income produced by an asset and the original capital cost (the price paid to buy the asset) or alternatively its current market value.*

Major Metropolitan Areas vs Rural Areas

In larger metropolitan areas, historics can be gathered for what the cumulative CAP rate has been. This can be retrieved from a knowledgeable broker and will help you determine potential asset valuations based upon trends for that location. This is supported with several comparable property NOI's and comparable sales in that area. This is highly capable in a big city. However, in a more rural area, trends may not be consistent and other methods of determining valuation may be necessary. In this case, you may need to look at alternative methods, like possibly what the price per unit has been for a comparable property. After we review the value equation, you will see how you may use the CAP rate and NOI to compute the assets' value.

Let us review capitalization rate (CAP).

We will use our (2) unit example in consideration of this property's purchase capitalization rate as well as it's net operating income (NOI).

CAP RATE TABLE

Take your NOI and divide it by your purchase price to equate CAP rate.

CAP RATE		
Purchase Price	$	150,000
Gross Income (Monthly)	$	2,550
Gross Income + Parking	$	30,600
Vacancy (5%)	$	1,530
Effective Gross Income	**$**	**29,070**
Property Taxes	$	1,612
Property Insurance	$	951
Property Manager Fees @ 7%	$	2,035
Other Operating Expenses	$	8,140
Total Operating Expenses	**$**	**12,738**
Net Operating Income (NOI)	**$**	**16,332**
CAP RATE		**10.88%**
C.R. Wesley		

CAP RATE = NOI / PURCHASE PRICE

0.1088 = $16332 / $150,000 or 10.88%

☞ *Notice how we can interchange data using this equation to arrive at the figure we are seeking. Example being, the NOI divided by the Cap Rate gives you the value of the property.*

☞ *To summarize, if you have two of the three figures using the value equation below, you can find the third or missing value.*

VALUE TABLE

VALUE = NOI/CAP RATE	
NOI	$ 16,332
CAP RATE	10.88%
VALUE	$ 150,000
C.R. Wesley	

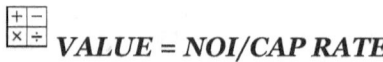
VALUE = NOI/CAP RATE

☞ *In chapter 7, you will learn about asset class. Please come back to this example and see what asset class this property would align with?*

When yuo determine the asset class, you should then confirm if the property aligns with a C Class location. When you are doing your valuations, these are questions you should be thinking about.

☞ *Hopefully, these questions are peaking your inquisitiveness...*

As mentioned previously in Chapter 5 regarding larger metropolitan areas and rural areas, we could use the value formula to find any value we are seeking.

☞ *If we have, NOI and purchase price, we can evaluate the CAP rate to see if this rate meets our expectations.*

☞ If we have the NOI and the CAP rate, we can see if the value is consistent with comparables. This could provide insight if our NOI is perhaps too high or if our CAP rate is too low...

☞ If we have purchase price and CAP rate, we can see if the computed NOI is accurate to the actuals from the income statement provided by the owner.

🚦 *This will be your red flag alert if things are not aligned! Here are some general tips as we are assessing asset value.*

Things to Check

- Is the property commercial or residential? Commercial property is 5 or more units. Utility costs for commercial property is generally higher than *residential property utilities (residential = 4 units or less).*

- *What is the age of the furnace (or boiler), roof, HVAC and water heater? Is there a well and septic system and what condition is it in? Will any of these need replacement or repair soon?*

  - *These are possible capital expenses. Capital expenses are advised to estimate at 1% of the properties' cost. This helps projections for the cash flow analysis. However capital expenditures can vary widely based upon deferred maintenance in conjunction with the cost of the property.*

    - *Example -A low cost property could have lots of deferred maintenance causing CAP X to be a much higher percentage than an annual 1% cost.*

Do your due diligence and consider this on a case-by-case scenario. Please plan accordingly.

- *Is the heating, electrical and water systems metered individually for each unit? This helps create better organization for managing liabilities and associating accurate expenditures to the units. Ideally tenants would have responsibility for their own utility costs.*
- *What are the current leases in place and when do they expire?*
  - *Try to get 3 years of rent rolls from the current owner to see the actual vacancy rates.*

As you are seeing, real estate investing can require much analyzing. Everything from the cash flow analysis to the comparable market value assessments on a property are important on every deal. The best investors are the ones that know how to evaluate these numbers efficiently and to walk away if the conditions are not in their favor. Be sure your assessment techniques are sound, and you stand by your method. Set your baselines as well as a system to evaluate these pointers every time.

Chapter 7
Finding Property

Finding properties can be hard work. As you can see, the process in locating good investments can require hard work. It is ideal that you have several sources that can lead you to a deal. One way to find properties is the multiple listing service (MLS). The MLS always has residential real estate properties for sale. Create a target price along with the criteria you are looking for in a property and make your phone calls.

For residential real estate, try websites like:

www.zillow.com

www.realtor.com

www.redfin.com

www.trulia.com

www.homesnap.com

For commercial real estate, try websites like:

www.loopnet.com

www.crexi.com

www.ten-x.com

www.brevitas.com

When you do call to confirm details on the property, ask the following questions:

- How long the owner has been trying to sell?
- Is the mortgage assumable for seller financing?
- How old is the roof?
- What is the condition of the HVAC?
- Are there any known repair issues?
- When do the leases expire?

- Does the basement have any leaks or dampness?
- Are there any known foundation issues?
- Have there been any oil leaks in the basement?
- Is the water source municipal or is there a well and septic system?
- Do you have an income statement showing revenue and operational expenses?

Sometimes the owners have income statements that they can send you, so be sure to inquire.

Alternative Methods of Locating Investments

💡 If you are looking to buy properties in a non-traditional way, when your bird dog sends you a lead, you can ask the seller if he or she is willing to do seller financing. Seller financing is a real estate agreement in which the seller accepts a monthly payment agreement instead of that agreement coming from a financial institution. You would pay the owner directly each month. Instead of applying for a conventional bank mortgage, the buyer signs an agreement with the seller for a down payment and a monthly fee for a specified period of time until the property is purchased outright. Seller financing is also known as owner financing and a purchase-money mortgage. You never know how creative a seller is willing to be in a sales transaction and sometimes you can find some great deals performing this strategy.

Another way to find properties is to buy from other investors or wholesalers. Investors can be a good source because investors may have great deals on hand that they are willing to let go. Wholesalers are strictly in the business of finding great deals and all they will need is your criteria.

Both are good lead sources. If you use this method and you are using traditional lending, you must ensure the home is in livable condition. Banks will not finance an unlivable residence.

> *Unlivable Definition -* A home is not habitable when it has serious problems that make staying in the home dangerous. Serious hazards such as inadequate plumbing, rodent infestations, or holes in the roof or walls are all examples that make a home unlivable.

💡 For sale by owner sites are also good options to check and are sometimes purchasable at a good discount. Be sure to try this avenue. You may find some motivated sellers.

💡 "Driving for dollars" is another method where you can locate deals. You may have learned this strategy if you have learned to bird dog. These could be vacant, dilapidated, or occupied properties with potential to add value. If you can correspond with the owner, you may have found your next investment! This is also a good source.

💡 Marketing your interests is another way to advise possible motivated sellers that you are interested in their property. Many investors adopt these techniques and reach out to people that may need their help. This marketing can be in the form of a letter, postcard, phone call or door knock...

Some of the motivation targeted in this type of lead source may include the following:

Divorce	Probate
Code Violations	Vacant
Dilapidated	Tax Delinquent
Pre-Foreclosure	Tired Landlord
Retiring Investors	Expired MLS
Bank REOs	Fire/Storm Damage
Job Loss	Relocation

☞ *Whether you are looking for motivated sellers, using the MLS, a broker/realtor, a bird dog, a wholesaler or you are locating sellers on your own, find the property that best fits your needs.*

<u>*You will have to define your strategy.*</u>

<u>*Remember you can look for:*</u>

1) Properties with little to no appreciation and high cash flow.

2) Properties that appreciate with less cash flow.

3) Properties with both moderate cash flow and moderate appreciation.

4) Properties with higher value potential that you will buy low, renovate, and hold.

Asset Class

This leads us to identifying asset class for your prospective investments. We have spoken about identifying the trends of the area where you are purchasing. Identifying this detail will require feedback from other local professionals and doing your research. There are services good for relaying this information. www.mashvisor.com has a service where they provide relative CAP rates throughout the US based upon relevant trends. Maybe this is something you should investigate if you are looking to purchase investments nationally. Overall, ideally CAP rates will relate to a properties asset class. Usually the properties asset class corresponds with that property's potential to appreciate.

Use the knowledge of asset class when gathering data to evaluate your valuations of a property. This can specifically relate to using the value formula from page 82, determining the missing value and recognizing a "red flag" or not. Let us review the asset classes, their respective capitalization rates and their investment characteristics.

ASSET CLASS TABLE

Class A – *Upper Class Asset – Typical CAP Rate 3%-5%*

- **High Appreciation/Low Cash Flow**

Class B – *Middle Class Asset – Typical CAP Rate 6%-8%*

- **Moderate-High Appreciation//Low-Moderate Cash Flow**

Class C – *Working Class Asset – Typical CAP Rate 9%-11%*

- **Low-Moderate Appreciation/Moderate-High Cash Flow**

Class D – *Impoverished Asset – Typical CAP Rate 12%+*

- **No Appreciation-Decline Potential/High Cash Flow**

Remember to assess the areas to determine if a property could be a C Class asset in a B Class area. What this refers to is identifying great opportunities with high value adding potential. A C Class asset in a B Class area is a investment with high potential returns. Possibly the owner is charging tenants lower rent as a C Class area would, but in fact the location could be earning higher rents because the property is in a B Class area.

These opportunities are high value and are great finds! This also happens when economic improvements occur in areas and begin to drive more economic growth. However, if the opportunity has not been seized by the property owner, maybe you can make an offer, gain ownership of the property and conduct your plan. Be sure to collect performance results to determine if there is an opportunity to be seized. Maybe a major employer in the area has went bankrupt and has laid off several employees so jobs are less abundant in the area. This is an example so you know to do your homework and not exclude factors that could affect your investments outcome. The opportunities are out there so seek them out! Eye of the tiger – champ!!

> *Note: Great finds await you. You may locate a C Class asset in a B Class area...This example can happen across any asset class. See example below...*
>
>> *Example – Rents in a 10-unit building are $700 per month and could be $800 per month with just some minor improvements to each unit. The improvements will cost $10,000. Once the improvements are completed the income will improve by $1000 per month. Therefore, the repair costs will pay off in 10 months with all future months being added income for years to come.*

Here are a few qualities of areas with higher potential assets. Good schools, reliable transportation, grocery stores, hospitals and banks are key ingredients for higher potential assets. Towns that have their own hospital is also a good sign of a neighborhood with more to offer – jobs being the key ingredient. Hospitals employ many people and the pay is typically a higher wage. A key and very important factor that big cities often pay less attention to is jobs. With an abundance of a thriving-high traffic economy, sometimes the essentials get overlooked. In smaller towns, you must evaluate the proximity of your property to where people are commuting for work. These factors are key in evaluating your prospective investments.

Finding properties to buy is not always an easy thing to do, but if you use the information provided, you will have many ideas of where to start your evaluations. Be ready to connect with owners when you come across properties where motivation is possible. County records can lead you in the right direction to locate contact information of the owner.

Maybe this will be a method you plan to deploy if you perhaps are going to send mailers to potential sellers.

Chapter 8

Depreciation and Taxes

As a rental property investor, it is important you understand the application of tax depreciation when filing your taxes. No discussion on real estate investing would be complete without an explanation on the applications of tax depreciation. Real estate depreciation is an income tax deduction that allows a taxpayer to recover the cost basis of their depreciating assets. Depreciation is essentially a non-cash deduction that defers the investor's taxable income. Many investors refer to it as a "phantom" expense because they are not actually writing a check. Depreciation is a tax deduction based on the possible decrease in the value of the asset due to natural wear and tear compared to the life expectancy of the tangible asset.

Real estate depreciation associates the costs to maintain material upkeep that the property incurs over time as a result of normal wear and tear. As a result of claiming the depreciation, the investor may increase cash flow from the property that may have been a greater tax loss, if the expense was not factored. There may be a benefit to deferring this yearly versus waiting until the asset is sold. You can decide how you will allocate your depreciation with your accountant based upon your investment strategy. This can help save you hundreds to thousands per year on taxes.

Consider The Property Tax

Often, investors base their purchases on current property taxes. Then, once a property renovation is complete, a higher property value may be applied, increasing the taxes. Be aware of this. Find out the state tax laws and possible tax changes post renovation. Incorporate the projected property tax estimates into your calculations.

If you are preparing to sell a property, review the utilization of a 1031 Exchange. If you are still reinvesting into the real estate market, you may be able to defer capital gains by utilizing a 1031 exchange. Follow up with your CPA for more details.

<u>1031 Exchange Definition</u>

A 1031 Exchange allows an investor to sell a property and then reinvest the proceeds into a new property, within a certain time limit. The property must be of like-kind and equal or greater value to defer all capital gain taxes.

Supplemental Tax

In some states, when purchasing a property, you are responsible for paying a supplemental tax. This is usually a local tax paid to your county tax assessor. In California, for example, you receive a supplemental tax bill to be paid in two payments. The amount due is a percentage of the previous owners' assessed value as compared to the price you paid for the property. This covers the difference in the assets previously assessed value and the current assessed value.

For example, if the previous owner paid $200,000 and you paid $400,000 for the same property, the property could be reassessed, and the new assessed value would be $400,000. Your local tax office would send you a supplemental tax bill due in two payments for a percentage of that $200,000 difference. This bill is in addition to your normal property tax bill, but thankfully it doesn't exist in every state.

It is important that you and your accountant are aware of reducing your yearly tax liability by associating the proper depreciation costs on your rental property. This is not mandatory, but it is an option if you would like to assess your depreciation costs yearly. If you would like to wait until the property is sold you could assess the depreciation, then. This is a key component in assessing your assets accordingly. Be sure to cover this discussion with your CPA.

Chapter 9

Exit Strategy

People enter the real estate investing business for the financial benefits. It's no secret that the whole point of purchasing investment properties is to make money through appreciation and generate income for years to come. No successful real estate investor enters the market without establishing an efficient and effective business plan. Be sure to have an exit strategy before purchasing any investment property. The best planning usually involves a strategy to follow the initial strategy. The plan after the plan or the exit plan.

An exit strategy is a plan in which the investor intends to remove themselves from the investment. Essentially, an exit strategy is a consideration to what the investor will do with the investment property. This is where your appreciation profit potential is executed. Be aware, that you make money when you buy! Hence, when you buy at an effective price, you reap the benefits of that purchase at the exit strategy.

Exit strategies should be planned as part of the original investment. For some investments you may start to consider an exit strategy once you have a clearer picture of how your portfolio is doing. Plans may change. Be prepared for flexibility and adaptive decision making in these instances. Good investors are nimble in deciphering the next best step. You may be certain that you want to purchase a property to add to your portfolio, without a concise plan on when you will exit. This is okay provided the entrance made sense from a number's standpoint and you are well informed on the location's potential. Without the exit strategy just be aware that you are taking more risks. You should always foresee an "end game" for the investment.

Determining an appropriate exit strategy not only will provide investors with a plan of action, but it will also minimize risks. When investors evaluate potential exit strategies before purchasing investment properties, they realize the risks associated with the investment and know how to better avoid them.

Having a specific exit strategy is crucial to success. The correct approach will result in maximized profits. It's never wise to enter into a deal without having a clear understanding of how you will profit from the property.

Having a financial goal and an exit strategy can save you thousands – if not millions – of dollars throughout your investing career.

As described before, equally important to the exit strategy is the entrance into an investment. Your entry point is vital in securing planned profits. Take precaution with this step and do not be hasty or anxious. Entering an asset too quickly without vetting the numbers can affect your gains in that asset's appreciation.

Understanding and choosing the right entrance and exit strategy will ultimately affect how successful you will be in your real estate investing career. You may have an exit strategy that is as short as 1 year or a strategy that is as long as 30 years. Do your best to keep your money growing and working for you. Know when your market is peaking to assess if you would want to exit. Know the tax advantages of your corporate structure and possible use of a 1031 exchange accordingly. Corporate structure relates to the entity you are operating under – LLC, C Corp, S Corp, LLP, etc....

Real estate markets rise and fall, so when assets are peaking, it is important to identify these intervals. Knowing when you are in a deficit is equally important. Be prepared for both and prepared to take appropriate action. However you apply your strategy, do your best to always make informed and calculated decisions to support your financial freedom.

Conclusion

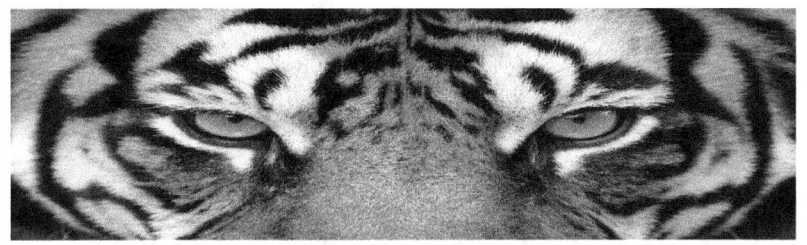

Be sure to have the eye of the tiger out there!! You are a champion! Buying rental properties can be a good or bad investment just like anything else. Making educated and calculated decisions are what will support you best. There are several rules of thumb for calculating expenses and cash flow that you have learned in this literature. You also need to know how to analyze rents in the area of your investment. (Try www.rentometer.com) Search rents and aesthetics of any comparable unit in proximity of your investment. Assess capital expenses and determine whether a big repair is a deal breaker or not. These are just friendly reminders.

Buying rental properties can be a satisfying way to make a side income or even a primary income as long as you go into it with proper preparation, and you do not believe the infomercial hype about instant wealth.

__We wish you great success!!__

This literature is brought to you by C.R. Wesley.

Please rate this literature online provided the vendor has a review feature.

We would appreciate your feedback and supportive rating if you found this book helpful.

Thank you and keep striving for growth.

See more of our literature in our Real Estate Knowledge Series by C.R. Wesley below.

We strive to give you the tools to educate you and lead you to greater success.

- Securing Grant Money– Step-by-Step Guide for First-Time Homebuyers by C.R. Wesley
- Acquiring Rental Property – Learning Your Options for Starting Your Investment Portfolio by C.R. Wesley
- Understanding Tax Lien and Tax Deed Investments – No Fluff by C.R. Wesley

ABOUT THE AUTHOR

Hello and thank you for selecting our literature as a resource.

I sincerely hope that it was helpful for you and has provided value to you and your current situation. My ambition is to provide knowledge to help you build success through self-development and education. There is knowledge, but knowledge means little without action. My intention is to provide the knowledge and give you actionable steps that you can implement into your life. My contribution will not be about me, but more about the information and how to use it. I will try to be concise and engaging while also keeping the information compact. Efficient for convenience, but impactful is the goal.

Some people have a diverse knowledge of these topics and others do not. I intend to help more of us have the common knowledge of material that will help make your life healthier. Much of our health starts in the mind. I intend to provide many materials that are all applicable in your self-growth. The applications of growth cover a wide variety.

My knowledge has started with extreme passion to be successful which transformed its way into my corporate atmosphere. Through self-education, enabling me to initiate conversations, and continue growth through interaction and continued education, I was able to grow myself tremendously over time. Real estate, stock market, entrepreneurship, personal growth, and leadership growth have been my experience.

My passion has always been for people and for providing a helpful means of growth. Hopefully, I can provide something inspirational, motivating, and impactful. I have always been "a sponge" of everything in my atmosphere. I aspire to share educational experiences with others for them to absorb. For some it will be a drip and for others it will be a waterfall. I will try to accommodate both, so everyone walks away with fruitful knowledge. I only ask that you pass on the positivity and healthy lifestyles to others as you grow.

Thank you for your time. C.R. Wesley

Thanks for reading! Please add a short review and let me know what you thought.